HYMN FAVORITES
FOR UKULELE

ISBN 978-1-4234-9917-6

HAL•LEONARD®
CORPORATION
7777 W. BLUEMOUND RD. P.O. BOX 13819 MILWAUKEE, WI 53213

In Australia Contact:
Hal Leonard Australia Pty. Ltd.
4 Lentara Court
Cheltenham, Victoria, 3192 Australia
Email: ausadmin@halleonard.com.au

Visit Hal Leonard Online at
www.halleonard.com

Abide with Me

Words by Henry F. Lyte
Music by William H. Monk

All Hail the Power of Jesus' Name

Words by Edward Perronet
Altered by John Rippon
Music by Oliver Holden

Be Thou My Vision

Traditional Irish
Translated by Mary E. Byrne

Crown Him with Many Crowns

Words by Matthew Bridges and Godfrey Thring
Music by George Job Elvey

Come, Thou Fount of Every Blessing

Words by Robert Robinson
Music from John Wyeth's *Repository of Sacred Music*

First note

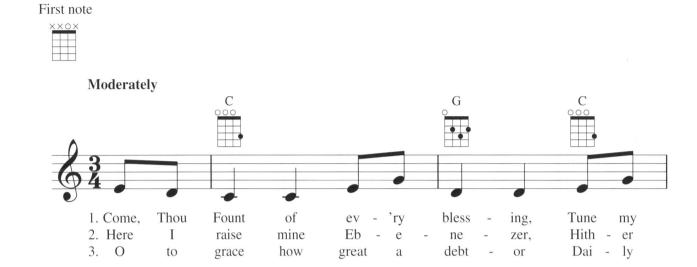

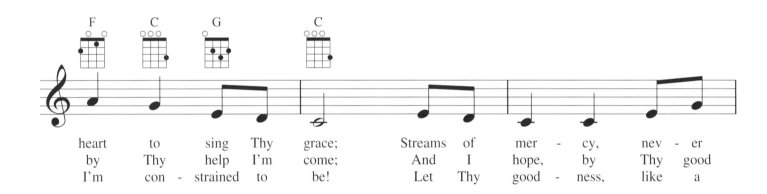

praise.   Teach me _____ some me - lo - dious
home.   Je - sus _____ sought me when a
Thee.   Prone to _____ wan - der, Lord, I

son - net, Sung by _____ flam - ing tongues a -
stran - ger, Wan - d'ring _____ from the fold of
feel _____ it, Prone to _____ leave the God I

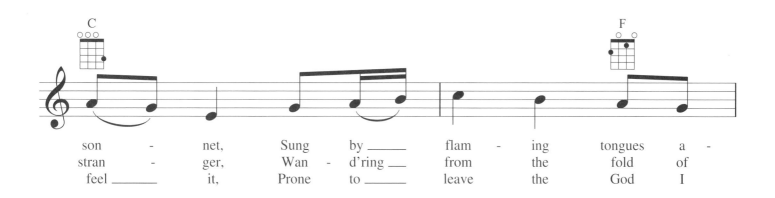

bove;   Praise the mount, I'm fixed up -
God;   He, to res - cue me from
love;   Here's my heart, O take and

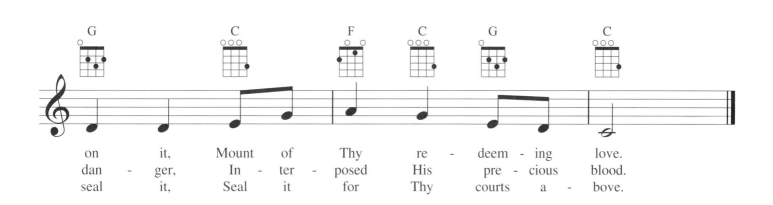

on it, Mount of Thy re - deem - ing love.
dan - ger, In - ter - posed His pre - cious blood.
seal it, Seal it for Thy courts a - bove.

Fairest Lord Jesus

Words from *Münster Gesangbuch*
Verse 4 by Joseph A. Seiss
Music from *Schlesische Volkslieder*

1. Fair - est Lord Je - sus, Rul - er of all na - ture,
2. Fair are the mead - ows, Fair - er still the wood - lands,
3. Fair is the sun - shine, Fair - er still the moon - light,
4. Beau - ti - ful Sav - ior! Lord __ of the na - tions!

O Thou of God and __ man the Son;
Robed in the bloom - ing __ garb of spring:
And all the twin - kling, __ star - ry host:
Son of __ God and __ Son of Man!

Thee will I cher - ish, Thee will I hon - or, Thou,
Je - sus is fair - er, Je - sus is pur - er, Who
Je - sus shines bright - er, Je - sus shines pur - er, Than
Glo - ry and hon - or, Praise, ad - o - ra - tion, Now

my soul's glo - ry, joy and crown. _____
makes the woe - ful heart to sing. _____
all the an - gels heav'n can boast. _____
and for - ev - er - more be Thine! _____

For the Beauty of the Earth

Words by Folliot S. Pierpoint
Music by Conrad Kocher

First note

Moderately

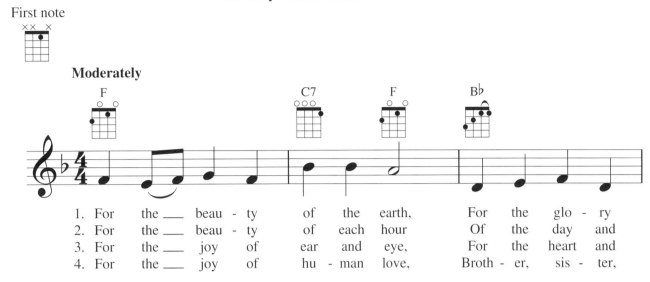

1. For the __ beau - ty of the earth, For the glo - ry
2. For the __ beau - ty of each hour Of the day and
3. For the __ joy of ear and eye, For the heart and
4. For the __ joy of hu - man love, Broth - er, sis - ter,

of the skies, For the __ love which from our birth
of the night, Hill and __ vale, and tree and flow'r,
mind's de - light, For the __ mys - tic har - mo - ny
par - ent, child, Friends on __ earth and friends a - bove,

Refrain

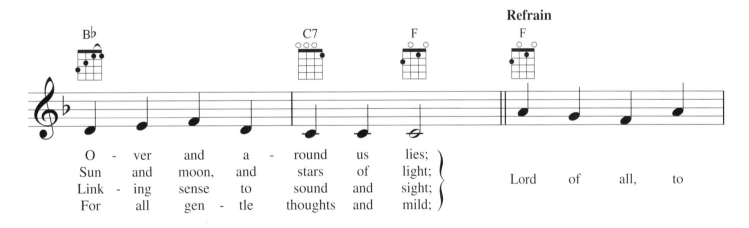

O - ver and a - round us lies; ⎫
Sun and moon, and stars of light; ⎬ Lord of all, to
Link - ing sense to sound and sight; ⎭
For all gen - tle thoughts and mild;

Thee we raise This our hymn of grate - ful praise.

Holy, Holy, Holy

Text by Reginald Heber
Music by John B. Dykes

How Firm a Foundation

Words from John Rippon's *A Selection of Hymns*
Early American Melody

First note

1. How ___ firm a foun - da - tion, ye saints of the
2. "Fear ___ not, I am with thee, O be not dis -
3. "When ___ through the deep wa - ters I call thee to
4. "When ___ through fier - y tri - als thy path - ways shall
5. "The ___ soul that on Je - sus still leans for re -

Lord, Is ___ laid for your faith in His ex - cel - lent
mayed, For ___ I am thy God and will ex still give thee
go, The ___ riv - ers of woe shall not thee o - ver -
lie, My ___ grace all - suf - fi - cient shall be thy sup -
pose, I ___ will not, I will not de - sert to its

Word! What more can He say than to you He hath
aid; I'll ___ strength - en and help thee, and cause thee to
flow; For ___ I will be with thee, thy trou - bles to
ply; The ___ flame shall not hurt thee; I on - ly de -
foes; That ___ soul, though all hell should en - deav - or to

said, To ___ you who for ref - uge to Je - sus have fled?
stand Up - held by My right - eous, om - ni - po - tent hand."
bless, And ___ sanc - ti - fy to thee thy deep - est dis - tress."
sign Thy ___ dross to con - sume, and thy gold to re - fine."
shake, I'll ___ nev - er, no, nev - er, no, nev - er for - sake."

I Need Thee Every Hour

Words by Annie S. Hawks
Music by Robert Lowry

First note

1. I need Thee ev-'ry hour, Most gra - cious _ Lord; No
2. I need Thee ev-'ry hour: Stay Thou _ near _ by; Temp-
3. I need Thee ev-'ry hour, In joy _ or _ pain; Come
4. I need Thee ev-'ry hour, Most Ho - ly _ One; O

ten - der voice like Thine Can peace _ af - ford.
ta - tions lose their pow'r When Thou _ art _ nigh.
quick - ly and a - bide, Or life _ is _ vain.
make me Thine in - deed, Thou bless - ed _ Son!

I

need Thee, O I need Thee; Ev - 'ry hour I need Thee! O

bless me now, my Sav - ior: I come _____ to Thee!

I Surrender All

Words by J.W. Van Deventer
Music by W.S. Weeden

First note

1. All to Je - sus I sur-ren - der; All to Him I free - ly give;
2. All to Je - sus I sur-ren - der; Hum - bly at His feet I bow,
3. All to Je - sus I sur-ren - der; Make me, Sav - ior, whol - ly thine;
4. All to Je - sus I sur-ren - der; Lord, I give my - self to Thee;

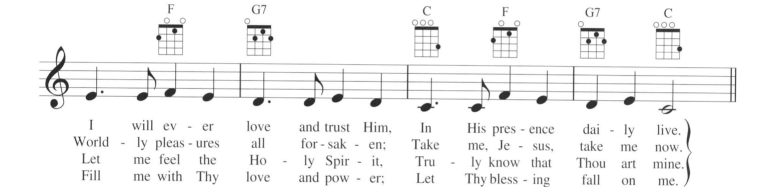

I will ev - er love and trust Him, In His pres - ence dai - ly live.
World - ly pleas - ures all for - sak - en; Take me, Je - sus, take me now.
Let me feel the Ho - ly Spir - it, Tru - ly know that Thou art mine.
Fill me with Thy love and pow - er; Let Thy bless - ing fall on me.

Refrain

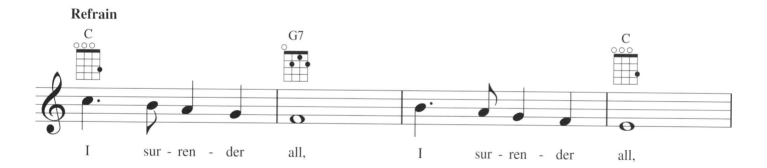

I sur - ren - der all, I sur - ren - der all,

All to Thee, my bless - ed Sav - ior, I sur - ren - der all.

It Is Well with My Soul

Words by Horatio G. Spafford
Music by Philip P. Bliss

First note

Gently

1. When peace like a riv - er at -
2. Though Sa - tan should buf - fet, though
3. My sin, O the bliss of this
4. And Lord, haste the day when the

tend - eth my way, When sor - rows like
tri - als should come, Let this blest as -
glo - ri - ous thought; My sin, not in
faith _____ shall be sight, The clouds be rolled

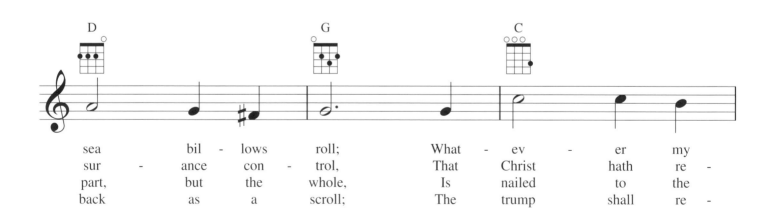

sea bil - lows roll; What - ev - er my
sur - ance con - trol, That Christ hath re -
part, but the whole, Is nailed to the
back as a scroll; The trump shall re -

Joyful, Joyful, We Adore Thee

Words by Henry van Dyke
Music by Ludwig van Beethoven, melody from *Ninth Symphony*
Adapted by Edward Hodges

First note

Brightly

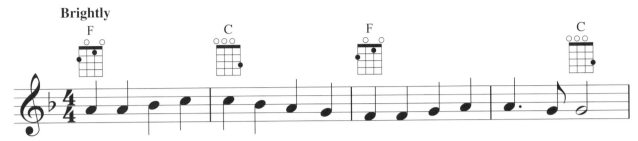

1. Joy - ful, joy - ful, we a - dore Thee, God of glo - ry, Lord of love;
2. All Thy works with joy sur-round Thee, Earth and heav'n re - flect Thy rays,
3. Thou art giv - ing and for - giv - ing, Ev - er bless-ing, ev - er blest,
4. Mor - tals, join the hap - py cho - rus Which the morn-ing stars be - gan;

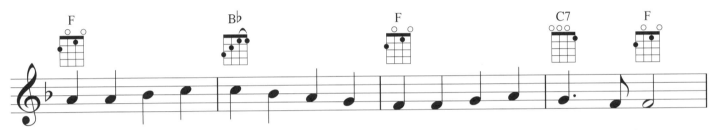

Hearts un - fold like flow'rs be - fore Thee, O - p'ning to the sun a - bove.
Stars and an - gels sing a - round Thee, Cen - ter of un - bro - ken praise.
Well-spring of the joy of liv - ing, O - cean depth of hap - py rest!
Fa - ther love is reign - ing o'er us, Broth - er love binds man to man.

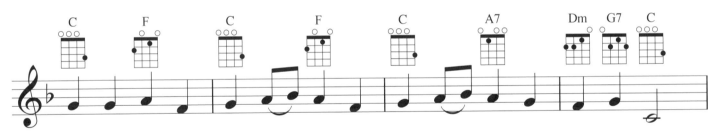

Melt the clouds of sin and __ sad - ness, Drive the __ dark of doubt a - way;
Field and for - est, vale and __ moun - tain, Flow - 'ry __ mead - ow, flash - ing sea,
Thou our Fa - ther, Christ our __ Broth - er, All who __ live in love are Thine;
Ev - er sing - ing, march we __ on - ward, Vic - tors __ in the midst of strife,

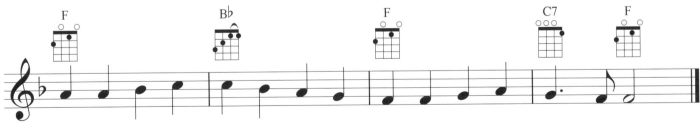

Giv - er of im - mor - tal glad - ness, Fill us with the light of day.
Chant - ing bird and flow - ing foun - tain, Call us to re - joice in Thee.
Teach us how to love each oth - er, Lift us to the joy di - vine.
Joy - ful mu - sic leads us sun - ward In the tri - umph song of life.

Just As I Am

Words by Charlotte Elliott
Music by William B. Bradbury

A Mighty Fortress Is Our God

Words and Music by Martin Luther
Translated by Frederick H. Hedge
Based on Psalm 46

First note

Majestically

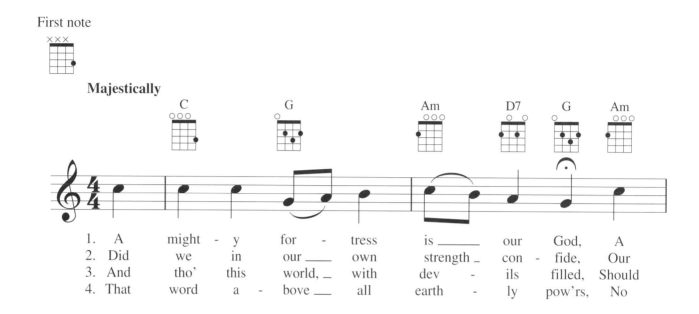

1. A might - y for - tress is _____ our God, A
2. Did we in our ____ own strength _ con - fide, Our
3. And tho' this world, _ with dev - ils filled, Should
4. That word a - bove ____ all earth - ly pow'rs, No

bul - wark nev - er fail - ing; Our
striv - ing would be los - ing, Were
threat - en to un - do _____ us, We
thanks to them, a - bid - eth; The

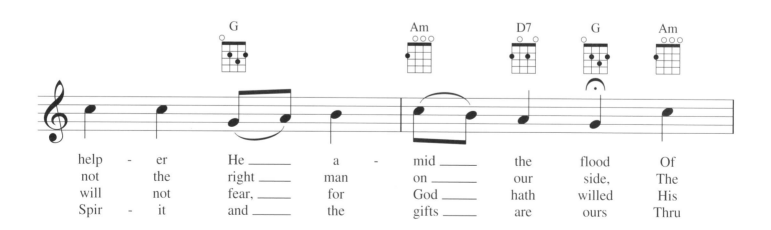

help - er He _____ a - mid _____ the flood Of
not the right ____ man on _____ our side, The
will not fear, ____ for God _____ hath willed His
Spir - it and ____ the gifts ____ are ours Thru

mor - tal ills pre - vail - ing. For still our an - cient
man of God's own choos - ing. Dost ask who that may
truth to tri - umph thru _____ us. The prince of dark - ness
Him who with us sid - eth. Let goods and kin - dred

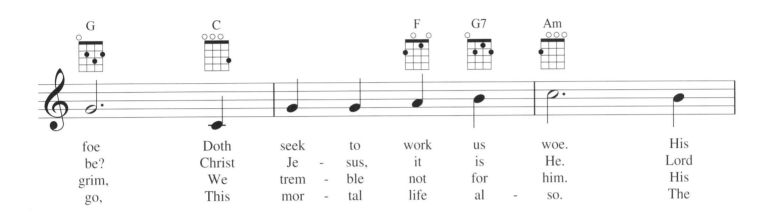

foe Doth seek to work us woe. His
be? Christ Je - sus, it is He. Lord
grim, We trem - ble not for him. His
go, This mor - tal life al - so. The

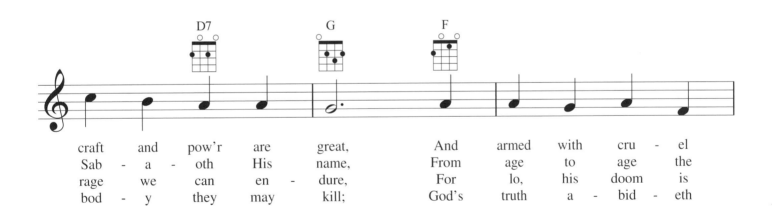

craft and pow'r are great, And armed with cru - el
Sab - a - oth His name, From age to age the
rage we can en - dure, For lo, his doom is
bod - y they may kill; God's truth a - bid - eth

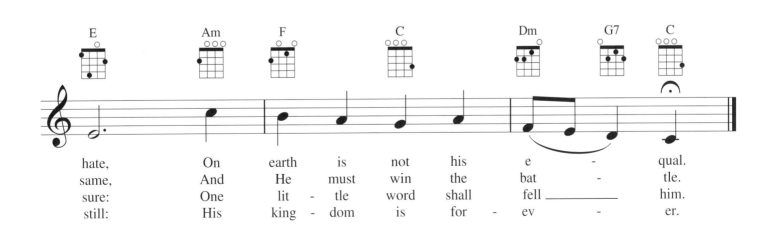

hate, On earth is not his e - qual.
same, And He must win the bat - tle.
sure: One lit - tle word shall fell _____ him.
still: His king - dom is for - ev - er.

My Faith Looks Up to Thee

Words by Ray Palmer
Music by Lowell Mason

First note

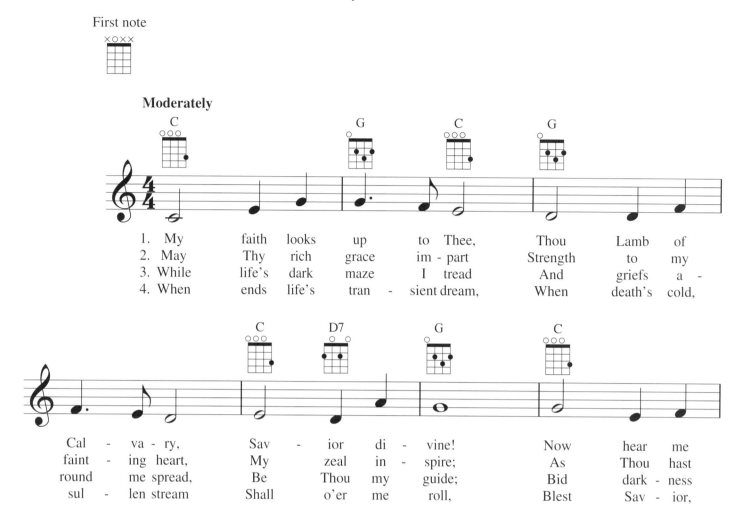

1. My faith looks up to Thee, Thou Lamb of
2. May Thy rich grace im - part, Strength to my
3. While life's dark maze I tread And griefs a -
4. When ends life's tran - sient dream, When death's cold,

Cal - va - ry, Sav - ior di - vine! Now hear me
faint - ing heart, My zeal in - spire; As Thou hast
round me spread, Be Thou my guide; Bid dark - ness
sul - len stream Shall o'er me roll, Blest Sav - ior,

while I pray, Take all my guilt a - way,
died for me, O may my love to Thee
turn to day, Wipe sor - row's tears a - way,
then, in love, Fear and dis - trust re - move;

O let me from this day Be whol - ly Thine!
Pure, warm and change - less be, A liv - ing fire!
Nor let me ev - er stray From Thee a - side.
O bear me safe a - bove, A ran - somed soul!

Nearer, My God, To Thee

Words by Sarah F. Adams
Music by Lowell Mason

O Worship the King

Words by Robert Grant
Music attributed to Johann Michael Haydn

Take My Life and Let It Be

Words by Frances R. Havergal
Music by Henry A. César Malan

Savior, Like a Shepherd Lead Us

Words from *Hymns for the Young*
Attributed to Dorothy A. Thrupp
Music by William B. Bradbury

First note

Flowing

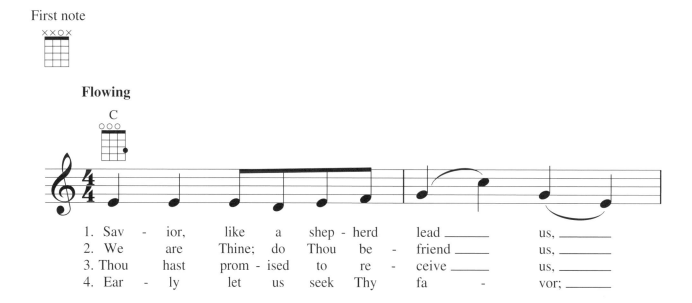

1. Sav - ior, like a shep - herd lead _____ us, _____
2. We are Thine; do Thou be - friend _____ us, _____
3. Thou hast prom - ised to re - ceive _____ us, _____
4. Ear - ly let us seek Thy fa - vor; _____

Much we need Thy ten - der care;
Be the Guard - ian of our way;
Poor and sin - ful though we be;
Ear - ly let us do Thy will;

In Thy pleas - ant pas - tures feed _____ us, _____
Keep Thy flock, from sin de - fend _____ us, _____
Thou hast mer - cy to re - lieve _____ us, _____
Bless - ed Lord and on - ly Sav - ior, _____

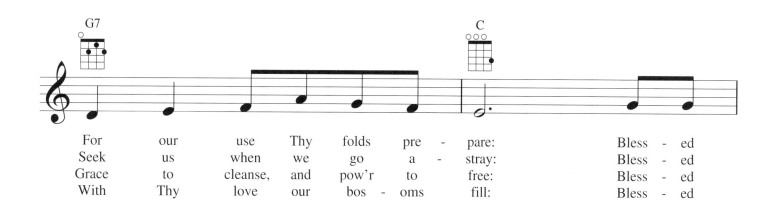

For our use Thy folds pre - pare: Bless - ed
Seek us when we go a - stray: Bless - ed
Grace to cleanse, and pow'r to free: Bless - ed
With Thy love our bos - oms fill: Bless - ed

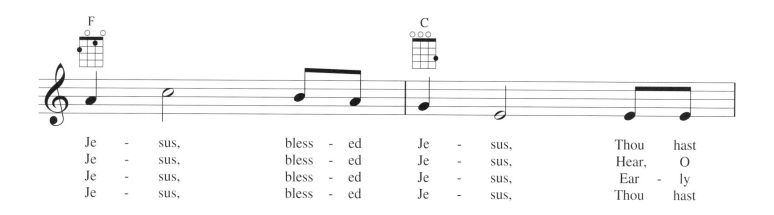

Je - sus, bless - ed Je - sus, Thou hast
Je - sus, bless - ed Je - sus, Hear, O
Je - sus, bless - ed Je - sus, Ear - ly
Je - sus, bless - ed Je - sus, Thou hast

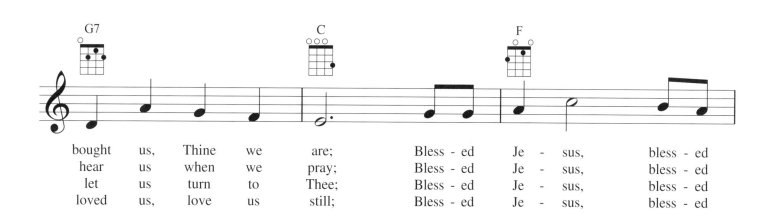

bought us, Thine we are; Bless - ed Je - sus, bless - ed
hear us, Thine when we pray; Bless - ed Je - sus, bless - ed
let us turn to Thee; Bless - ed Je - sus, bless - ed
loved us, love us still; Bless - ed Je - sus, bless - ed

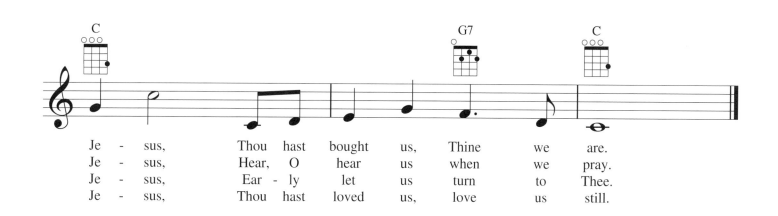

Je - sus, Thou hast bought us, Thine we are.
Je - sus, Hear, O hear us when we pray.
Je - sus, Ear - ly let us turn to Thee.
Je - sus, Thou hast loved us, love us still.

This Is My Father's World

Words by Maltbie D. Babcock
Music by Franklin L. Sheppard

First note

Warmly

1. This ____ is my Fa - ther's world, And ____
2. This ____ is my Fa - ther's world, The ____
3. This ____ is my Fa - ther's world, O ____

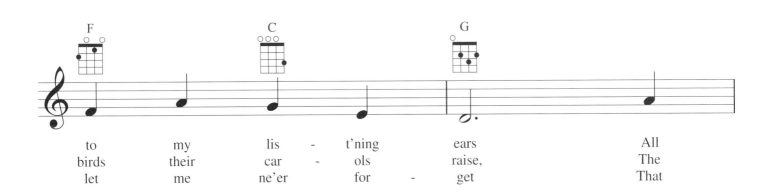

to my lis - t'ning ears All
birds their car - ols raise, The
let me ne'er for - get That

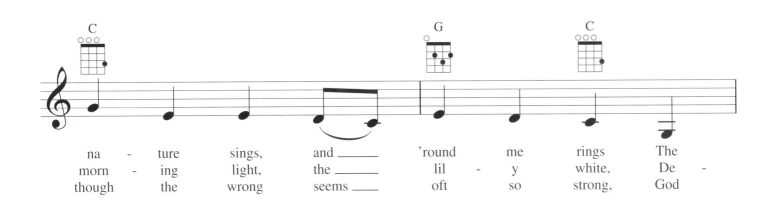

na - ture sings, and ____ 'round me rings The
morn - ing light, the ____ lil - y white, De -
though the wrong seems ____ oft so strong, God

mu -	sic	of	the _____	spheres.	This
clare _____	their	Mak -	er's _____	praise.	This
is _____	the	Rul -	er _____	yet.	This

is	my	Fa - ther's	world:	I _____	rest	me	in	the
is	my	Fa - ther's	world:	He _____	shines	in	all	that's
is	my	Fa - ther's	world:	The _____	bat - tle	is	not

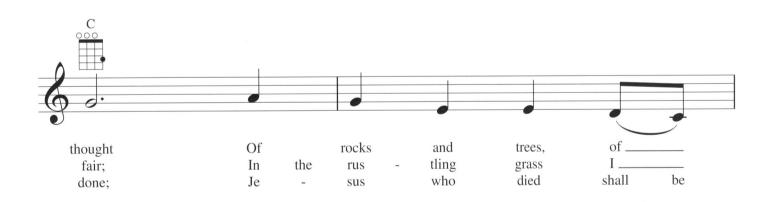

thought	Of	rocks	and	trees,	of _____
fair;	In the	rus - tling	grass	I _____
done;	Je - sus	who	died	shall	be

skies	and	seas,	His	hand _____	the	won - ders _____	wrought.
hear	Him	pass,	He	speaks _____	to	me	ev - 'ry - where.
sat - is - fied,	And	earth _____	and	heav'n	be _____	one.

To God Be the Glory

Words by Fanny J. Crosby
Music by William H. Doane

in.
ceives. }
see.

Praise the Lord! Praise the Lord! Let the

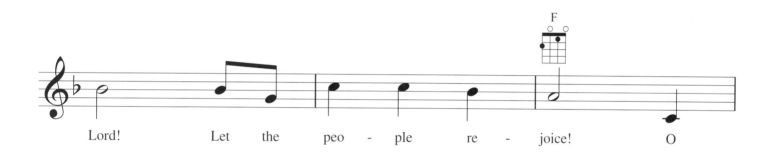

earth hear His voice! Praise the Lord! Praise the

Lord! Let the peo - ple re - joice! O

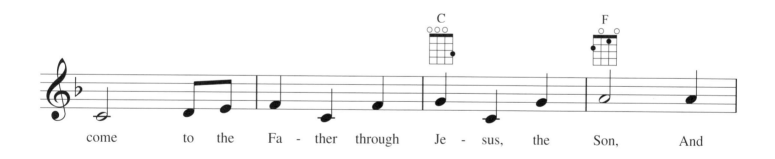

come to the Fa - ther through Je - sus, the Son, And

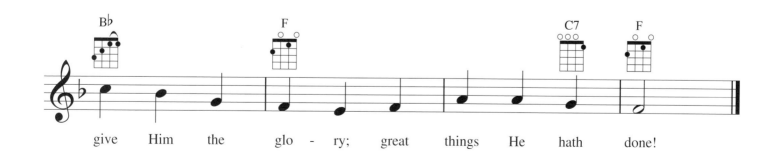

give Him the glo - ry; great things He hath done!

What a Friend We Have in Jesus

Words by Joseph M. Scriven
Music by Charles C. Converse

First note

Warmly

1. What a Friend we have in Je - sus,
2. Have we tri - als and temp - ta - tions?
3. Are we weak and heav - y - lad - en,

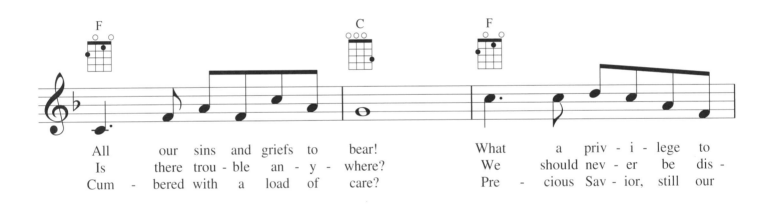

All our sins and griefs to bear!   What a priv - i - lege to
Is there trou - ble an - y - where?   We should nev - er be dis -
Cum - bered with a load of care?   Pre - cious Sav - ior, still our

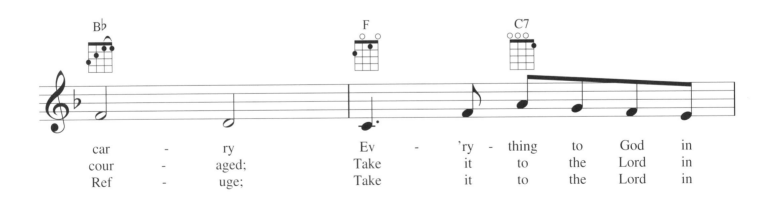

car - ry   Ev - 'ry - thing to God in
cour - aged;   Take it to the Lord in
Ref - uge;   Take it to the Lord in

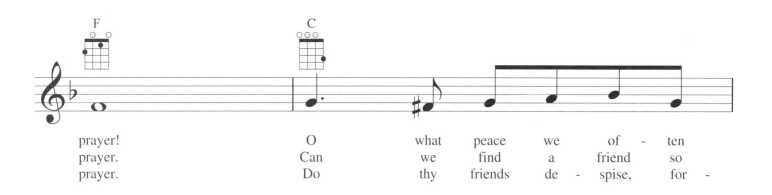

prayer!   O   what   peace   we   of - ten
prayer.   Can   we   find   a   friend   so
prayer.   Do   thy   friends   de - spise,   for -

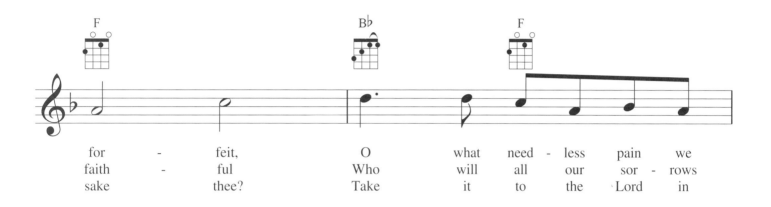

for - feit,   O   what   need - less   pain   we
faith - ful   Who   will   all   our   sor - rows
sake   thee?   Take   it   to   the   Lord   in

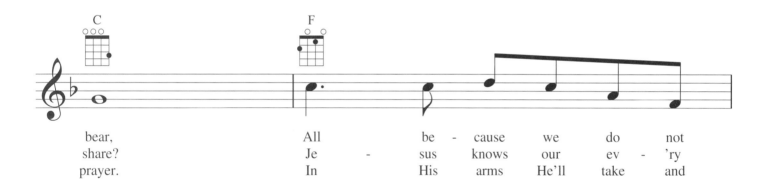

bear,   All   be - cause   we   do   not
share?   Je - sus   knows   our   ev - 'ry
prayer.   In   His   arms   He'll   take   and

car - ry   Ev - 'ry - thing   to   God   in   prayer!
weak - ness;   Take   it   to   the   Lord   in   prayer.
shield   thee;   Thou   wilt   find   a   sol - ace   there.

When I Survey the Wondrous Cross

Words by Isaac Watts
Music arranged by Lowell Mason
Based on Plainsong